MARY ELTING

WITH RACHEL FOLSOM AND ROBERT MOLL

VOLCANOES

AND

EARTHQUAKES

▲ ▲ ▲

ILLUSTRATED BY COURTNEY

SIMON AND SCHUSTER BOOKS FOR YOUNG READERS

Published by Simon & Schuster Inc.

New York ▲ London ▲ Toronto ▲ Sydney ▲ Tokyo ▲ Singapore

THE TALKING POT

One Saturday morning in 1943, ten-year-old Cresencio Pulido began to feel more and more frightened. He was hearing strange noises. Muttering sounds came from a big, pot-shaped depression in the middle of the cornfield where his father was ploughing. Old people often said that the pot talked to itself. But this morning the noises were louder.

While his father ploughed, Cresencio was supposed to watch the family's small flock of sheep and keep them from wandering away. Today the sheep seemed nervous. Each time the pot talked, the lambs huddled close to their mothers.

Suddenly, the pot gave a very loud snort, and a jet of white smoke rose out of it. Then, with a sound like thunder, the earth cracked open in a straight line across the pot.

"Go home!" Cresencio's father called.

The earth began to hiss now, and when

Cresencio turned, he saw black smoke rise from the crack. Fiery streaks shot up through the smoke, and sparks set a tree on fire. The ground began to tremble. Quickly, his father unhitched his ox from the plough and followed Cresencio home to their village, where he told people what had happened.

Cresencio Pulido and his father were terrified that Saturday. But afterward they felt proud in a way. They were among the few people in the world who have ever seen the exact beginning of a new volcano. After they left, the baby volcano kept spitting out a thick cloud and began tossing big rocks into the air. The cloud was not the kind that brings rain. It was made of tiny rock particles somewhat like the ash from a fire. Some of this ash fell back in a heap around the old talking pot, and in a little while it had become a cone-shaped hill 10 feet tall.

The new volcano soon got the name Parícutin (pronounced par-EE-coo-teen) because that was the name of the Mexican village where Cresencio and his family lived. Almost everyone in the village decided it wasn't safe to stay there. But on Sunday morning Cresencio's father went back for his ox and the donkeys he had left in his field. In the night the cone-shaped heap of ash had grown. It was at least 30 feet high now. By noon the cone was 100 feet high.

News of the volcano spread, and people came from miles away to watch. Suddenly that afternoon they saw a black stream burst from the foot of the cone and flow slowly across the field. The stream was made of *lava*—rock so hot that it had melted into a thick liquid.

Day after day the volcano cone grew taller, and ash began to bury the village of Parícutin. Now the lava flowed more quickly. Before long it reached a nearby town, pushed into a large stone church, and filled it completely. Only the bell tower stuck out. Everyone had already left the village and the town. By now most of their homes and fields had disappeared under ash or lava, but not one person had been hurt.

Parícutin went on erupting for nine years and twelve days before it grew quiet and the lava hardened in the *crater*—the funnel-shaped depression at its top. The volcano was now more than 1,300 feet high. Where had all this new rock come from? Before the eruption, a pool of very hot melted rock called *magma* had formed deep under the Earth's surface. Magma is what scientists call lava while it is still underground. Because magma is a liquid, it is lighter than the solid rock around it.

So it began to rise, pushing and melting its way up through any breaks or weak places above it. When it reached a spot just beneath the cornfield, it forced its way out, and the ground cracked with a terrible bang.

When the earth finally burst open, why did bits of magma froth up into the air? For the same reason that bubbles of soda squirt out of a pop bottle when you shake it and then take off the cap. Steam and other gases were dissolved in the magma the way carbon dioxide gas is dissolved in soda pop. While the cap is on the bottle, the gas stays in the soda. The earth's crust acted like the cap on the underground chamber full of magma—it kept the gas and water mixed into the liquid rock.

When the molten rock burst through the crack in the cornfield, gas-filled bubbles of magma expanded with such great force that they exploded upward and broke into tiny pieces. Some of the bits were as fine as dust. Larger bits of ash were the size of rice or peas. Still larger bits called *cinders* were as big as Ping-Pong balls.

A great deal of gas was concentrated in the magma that first exploded in clouds of ash. But deeper underground the magma was not so gassy. Instead of exploding, it just flowed out of the volcano in streams of thick, sticky lava.

What about the strange sounds that scared Cresencio before Parícutin erupted? Volcanoes usually give some sort of warning that the hot, rising magma is about to break through the earth's surface. The ground shudders and shakes as rock underneath it snaps and creaks. So it's no wonder that the old talking pot in the cornfield muttered and complained.

TAMING A VOLCANO

At two o'clock one winter night in 1973, a phone call from a neighbor awakened Magnus Magnusson.

"Magnus, there's a house on fire!"

Magnus looked out the window and saw a red glow in the sky. "No!" he cried. "It's an eruption!"

A new volcano had just been born half a mile from a town on the tiny island called Heimaey (pronounced HAY-may) off the coast of Iceland.

A few hours earlier, when Magnus went to bed, he had no idea that a gigantic plume of magma had risen from 8 miles beneath the earth to a spot just outside his town. Now the earth had split open in a mile-long gash, and a curtain of red-hot lava spurted 500 feet into the air.

Magnus, who was mayor of the town, acted quickly. By eight o'clock in the morning, boats had taken almost 5,000 people from Heimaey to safety on the mainland. All the chickens went by boat, too. Sheep got special treatment—they were flown out.

About 300 people stayed behind, hoping they could do something to save their town. Hot ash that looked like fine black gravel fell in a dark blizzard that buried some of their homes. Lava flowed toward town, making a tinkling sound. Slowly, it covered and burned building after building in its path. Worst of all, lava crept toward the island's harbor. If it flowed much farther, it would close the mouth of the harbor, and hundreds of fishermen would have nowhere to bring their catch.

How could the harbor be saved? Only by stopping the lava—and such a thing seemed impossible. But a scientist came up with a plan for doing just that. Pour cold water on it, he said. Pour on so much that the molten rock will cool and harden. The solid rock will then dam the flow and make the lava change direction—away from the harbor and toward the open sea.

At first people laughed. Stop a volcano? What a crazy idea! But the plan went ahead. Crews of workers started hosing down the lava with seawater, while people all over Iceland watched on television. Before long, the crews got help from a ship with a powerful pump.

A skin of hardened rock formed on top

of the cooling lava. When it was 2 inches thick, it could hold a person's weight. So the pumping crews walked out on top and laid down huge pipes. Now they could pour water over acres of hot rock. Soon the crust was thick enough to support a bulldozer, and the heavy machines began to make roads across the growing stretch of rough rock.

The crust was cool enough for the crews to walk on, even though rivers of red-hot lava still flowed underneath. But if they stood still for more than thirty seconds,

the soles of their boots sometimes melted or even caught fire. Still the heat wasn't all bad. After work, the pumping crews sometimes broiled steaks over a pit of glowing ash.

The lava fighters had to watch out for *volcanic bombs*—large globs of molten rock that shot up hundreds of feet. In the air, the globs cooled and formed a hard skin. Sometimes the gases inside made them explode like firecrackers. When they hit the ground, they often cracked open, and their still-molten insides splattered out.

Bombs the size of chairs sometimes flew a quarter of a mile. Luckily, they never hit anybody. One man got so used to the bombs that he picked up a small one, broke it open, and used it to light a cigar.

Week after week the efforts to save Heimaey's harbor went on. The molten rock piled up into a long black hill like an arm reaching into the sea. If it reached out another 150 feet, it would form a dam all the way across the entrance to the harbor. Then, just in time, the lava stopped. The people of Iceland had done what no one had ever done before. They had kept a major flow of lava from causing a catastrophe.

When the townspeople came back to Heimaey, they carted away millions of tons of the black ash and then used the rest to repave all their streets. Fishermen liked the new shape of the harbor because the long arm of lava gave it much better protection from the sea. And everyone liked the new heating system that used the lava to supply steam that kept the entire town warm.

Years have past since the eruption on Heimaey, but underneath the hardened surface, the rock is still molten. If you dig down a few inches into the ash and bury bread dough, a loaf will be ready to eat in a couple of hours.

THE GLOWING AVALANCHE

In the spring of 1902, people who lived on the island of Martinique in the Caribbean Sea began to feel uncomfortable. A smell like rotten eggs was drifting down from Mount Pelée (pronounced pell-AY), a cone-shaped volcano that rose above the city of St. Pierre. From time to time, the earth shook. Then a small eruption dumped several inches of light gray ash on the ground. The ash looked like snow, and it muffled the sounds of carriages in the streets. Finally, on the second of May, the silence was broken by several thunderous eruptions, followed by lightning storms.

The people of St. Pierre were frightened, but no one left the city. Animals, however, were growing restless. Ants and centipedes crawled out of the ground. Hundreds of poisonous snakes slithered down the mountainside into the city. Still, almost no one left.

Then on the morning of May 8, two huge clouds blasted out of the volcano. A black one shot straight up with a terrible roar and spread across the entire sky. The other was violet-gray, and so hot that it sparkled and glowed. This one rolled down the mountain at 100 miles an hour. In only two minutes it reached St. Pierre, destroying everything in its path.

The sparkling cloud was made up of steam, poisonous gases and ash. Scientists call such a cloud a *glowing avalanche* or a *fiery cloud*. It ripped off all the roofs in the city, knocked many stone buildings flat, and turned trees into charcoal. It picked up a huge statue and flung it 50 feet. Iron bars were bent like pretzels. Within a few seconds, the hot, poisonous cloud killed almost 30,000 people. Only a few in that entire large city were left alive.

One who escaped was a girl named Harviva. Miraculously, she managed to sail her brother's small boat to a nearby sea cave, where she and her friends used to play pirate. The last thing Harviva could remember was the great hissing sound when the super-heated avalanche hit the water. Two days later she was rescued from her boat, which had drifted far from shore.

Another survivor of the volcano couldn't get away—he was a prisoner in a dungeon built partly underground. The thick walls of the dungeon protected him, and the one tiny window faced away from the fiery cloud. A few days after the eruption, when the ash was cool enough to walk on, rescuers heard his cries for help. Later he was pardoned, went to the United States, and traveled around as an exhibit with the Barnum and Bailey Circus.

Soon after the eruption, a team of scientists came to study the ruins of St. Pierre. All of the destruction, they discovered, had been caused by the hot cloud—no lava had flowed from the volcano. But something about the cloud puzzled them. Why had it rushed down the mountain instead of blasting straight up like most volcanic clouds? They couldn't agree. Then one day when they were on a sailboat offshore, the volcano erupted again. As they watched, another glowing avalanche rolled down the side of the mountain, heading straight toward them. But just before it reached the boat, the cloud stopped advancing and began to rise.

A look at this second glowing avalanche helped scientists figure out why the cloud had rushed downhill. When the volcano erupted, it spewed out particles of ash mixed with gases. For a few minutes the mixture acted just like a heavy liquid, and so it poured down the mountainside. Then the solid bits began to fall out of the cloud, and the light, hot gases rose and floated away. That was why the frightened scientists in their boat lived to write their story.

Pelée used up most of its power in fierce explosions. But a few months after the big eruptions ended, the volcano put on one more amazing act. A great, thick tower of rock began to rise out of the crater. For six weeks the tower kept growing —50 feet higher every day. When at last it stopped rising, it was 1,000 feet tall. If some of its top had not crumbled away as it grew, the tower would have been almost half a mile tall!

This is what happened: When the glowing avalanches were over, the magma that remained beneath the crater was still thick but filled with much less gas than before. So instead of exploding, it pushed slowly upward, like toothpaste squeezing from a tube; and it hardened as it reached the air.

Pelée's tower gradually fell apart and tumbled back into the crater. But towers of much harder lava have formed in the craters of other volcanoes. A very tall one in Africa, called Ziwi spire, has been standing for fifteen million years.

FOUNTAINS OF FIRE

"What was that?" shouted Marty Godchaux, who was camping with a group of students in the national park on the island of Hawaii. It was almost two o'clock in the morning in March, 1984, and the ground had shaken, waking everyone up. Marty, a scientist who studies volcanoes, suddenly realized there was a red glow in the sky. "Kilauea must be erupting!"

Marty and her students had their campsite on the side of Mauna Loa (pronounced mow-na-LO-ah), the largest active volcano on Earth. Kilauea (pronounced kill-oo-WAY-ah), not far away, is smaller, newer, and one of the most active volcanoes in the world.

"It's not Kilauea!" cried one of the students. "It's Mauna Loa!"

For nine years Mauna Loa had been quiet. No one expected it to erupt so soon. But sure enough, tall fountains of lava were shooting out of the summit. This was going to be exciting.

Marty's group stayed up all night making careful observations and taking hundreds of photographs of the fire fountains, which were more than 800 feet high. The next morning park rangers flew by in a helicopter and asked them to leave. A fast-moving river of lava was only a quarter-mile from their campsite. So they packed up their gear and ran down the mountain, ahead of the stream of red-hot molten rock.

Why wasn't Marty afraid to spend the night on the side of an erupting volcano? She knew that Hawaiian volcanoes never explode violently when they erupt, and no one has ever died in an eruption there.

Hawaiian eruptions are quiet because the lava flows easily out of the crater or through cracks in the volcano's sides. This kind of lava is made up of certain minerals, such as iron, that melt into a rather thin liquid. The thick, sticky lava from Parícutin was made of different minerals that flow slowly when they melt. In Hawaii some of the thin lava shoots up out of the crater, but most of it just drizzles downhill like wax dripping down the side of a candle. Over the last million years, the drizzly eruptions have created enormously wide volcanoes with gentle slopes.

Scientists like Marty love to study Hawaiian volcanoes. Sometimes they can even predict an eruption. When a volcano is about to erupt, it bulges near the top, because magma is pushing up from below. To detect a bulge, scientists use an instrument called a *tilt meter*. The bulge tilts one end of the meter up. When this happens very quickly, scientists know that the volcano may burst open soon.

At the beginning of an eruption, when there is great pressure inside, spurts of lava called *fire fountains* often shoot up into the air. Some of them reach higher than the highest skyscraper. Streams of lava from the *caldera*—an oversized crater—or from cracks in the side of the volcano flow quickly down to the ocean. Rivers of lava can move 30 or 40 miles an hour.

The top of the red-hot river often cools and forms a hard black crust. Beneath the crust the lava stays hot and keeps on streaming downhill. After the eruption finally stops, the liquid lava drains out, leaving tunnels called *lava tubes*. Some are several miles long and big enough to walk through. The hot rock in these tunnels often cools into wormlike strings that hang from the ceiling.

Wearing shiny outfits like space suits to protect them from the heat, scientists can walk up to the very edge of a lava stream, stick in an iron rod, and pull out a glob of molten rock. When it cools and hardens, they can figure out what minerals are in it. Sometimes a big hunk of black, hardened lava will float downstream like a raft on a fiery river. Once a scientist wanted to see how fast a particular stretch of lava was flowing. So he hopped on one of these solid rafts while someone clocked his trip downstream.

Some scientists think that the island of Hawaii was formed by a hot spot deep in the Earth under the Pacific Ocean. An enormous column of magma rose from the hot spot, pushed, and melted its way up through the crust of the Earth, then burst out beneath the water. Piling higher and higher, the magma finally broke through the surface of the ocean and the island was born.

Thirteen hundred years ago, when people first came to Hawaii in small boats, eruptions of Mauna Loa probably guided them to their new home. A red glow from the tall volcano was visible for hundreds of miles. The new settlers found two kinds of lava. One flowed quickly and hardened into smooth rock that was comfortable to walk on. They called it *pahoehoe* (pronounced pah-HOY-hoy). The other kind moved much more slowly and hardened into sharp, jagged rock. They called it *aa* (pronounced AH-ah), because "Ah! ah!" is what they cried out when walking on it hurt their feet. These Hawaiian words have become the scientific names for the two kinds of lava.

THE FLATTENED FOREST

The volcano called Mount St. Helens had been asleep for more than a hundred years, but in mid-May, 1980, it was about to wake up. The earth near the base of the mountain trembled. The old crater at its top burped out puffs of steam. But that wasn't what fascinated the scientists who had come to watch and wait for an eruption. They were measuring a huge bulge that was growing on the side of the mountain. The soil and rock had swelled out like a giant blister more than 300 feet high and a mile long, and it was still swelling about 5 feet a day. What was pushing it? Magma, said the scientists, and very explosive magma at that. The super-hot molten rock in the throat of the volcano was loaded with gas and water, and it was very thick stuff—a combination that meant big trouble.

Everyone expected that the bulge would explode upward at any moment. It didn't. Instead it just broke away and slid downhill, leaving a gigantic hole in the side of the mountain. Straight out of the hole rose a great, billowing black cloud of ash, gas and steam. At the same time, grayish ash and steam blasted out sideways in an immense cloud that poured downhill at 300 miles an hour toward a great forest of tall trees. The powerful blast tore off branches, and the gritty ash scoured away the bark, leaving tree trunks completely bare. In just fifteen minutes, the whole forest toppled as if a giant machine had mowed it down. Tens of thousands of dead trunks, some as big around as a bulldozer tire, lay on the ground.

Meanwhile, the bulge that had slid downhill turned into an avalanche. It roared on and on into a river valley, and left it filled with piles of mud, ash, fallen trees and rock 600 feet deep.

Heat from the eruption soon melted the snow on the top of the volcano. Meltwater and steam were mixed with ash, and before long a great stream of mud began flowing downhill. It picked up earth, rocks and trees as it swelled into a flood that shattered bridges and washed houses away.

Just before the eruption, two scientists in a small plane were flying around the top of the volcano. "I guess nothing's going to happen today," said one of them. At that moment, the other scientist, who was looking out of the opposite window, gave a frightened gasp. The great black cloud suddenly burst out below them. This was no place for an airplane! Sharp bits of ash could ruin its engine. The pilot turned and headed for the airport in Yakima, Washington, 90 miles away. But the dark cloud was spreading in that same direction so fast it would catch up with the plane. The pilot had to take a different route to reach the airport safely.

In a few minutes the sky over Yakima was so dark that streetlights had to be turned on. When the scientists finally landed there, they found a carpet of ash 5 inches deep everywhere. The ash stuck wherever it fell. Snowplows had to clear the city streets. In fields nearby ash clung to the grass; and later, when hay-cutting time came, it dulled the blades of the machines. Some crops were ruined, but fruit trees were actually helped. Minerals in the volcanic ash fertilized the earth. The nectarines that autumn were huge and very sweet.

After the eruption, scientists began watching for any sign of what was still going on inside the volcano. Finally, they predicted there would soon be another outburst, but just a small one this time. They were right! Since May, 1980, they have studied each little twitch and gasp in Mount St. Helens, and they have been able to predict almost every small new eruption. Now they hope that, someday, it will be possible to predict all of the really dangerous ones.

THE ISLAND THAT BLEW ITS HEAD OFF

Sidney Baker was eleven years old in 1883 when he learned about volcanoes—but not from a book. He didn't go to school that year. Instead, his father, who was captain of a sailing ship, took him on a long sea voyage. They were halfway around the world and headed for home in the United States when an island volcano called Krakatoa (pronounced kra-ka-TOE-ah) erupted.

"It blew its head off," Sidney said, "and practically the whole island went up in the air."

A tremendous cloud of ash rose 50 miles high. The sky turned darker than night. People 3,000 miles away heard the blast, and Sidney's ears ached from the noise. Scariest of all was the lightning. It flashed and ran in giant streaks and fiery chains through the ash cloud.

Luckily, Captain Baker's ship was not harmed by the eruption. Most of the blast and the dense cloud had traveled away from the place where he had anchored. In other places hot ash fell 3 feet deep on ships' decks. It stuck like glue to the masts and sails. It crept down inside sailors' shirts and up their pant legs, and the air was so thick with dust that everything disappeared in absolutely black darkness. A lighted lantern held at arm's length was invisible.

When the sky finally cleared, sailors saw pumice floating all around. *Pumice* is a kind of hardened lava so full of gas bubbles that it looks like a sponge. The bubbles make it light enough to float on water. Some of the floating pumice chunks were as big as rowboats, and sailors actually hopped down off their ships and walked on them.

After the dreadful eruption ended, Captain Baker set sail. Before long, he told Sidney, they would pass a town called Anjer (pronounced AN-YER) on the coast of an island near Krakatoa. But he was wrong. Anjer had completely disappeared. A great wave, more than 130 feet high, had swept over it and washed away every house, every wagon, many animals, even big pieces of machinery.

A few people had seen the wave coming toward shore, like a tall, black, moving wall. They were close to a hill, and they ran to the top, where they were safe. One man, a little slower than the others, threw his arms around a banana tree just as the water hit him. He held on while the wave tore off all his clothes and left him standing naked when it rolled back. Everyone who hadn't run away was drowned.

What was this gigantic wave, and where did it come from? Scientists call it by its Japanese name—*tsunami* (pronounced sue-NA-mee). Waves of this kind used to be called *tidal waves*, but tsunamis have nothing to do with the tides. The Krakatoa tsunami began after the eruption stopped. By then the volcano had flung out so much magma that it left an enormous hole a half-mile deep in the ocean floor. Seawater poured into the hole, then sloshed out, then in and out again. At the same time, the ocean floor heaved upward and formed two new islands close to Krakatoa. Together, the heaving and the sloshing started the great ocean wave that swept Anjer away.

Neighboring islands felt the full power of the Krakatoa tsunami, and many thousands of people who lived close to the shore were killed. In one harbor the wave

picked up a large ship, carried it along a river valley, and set it down 2 miles from the sea. In other places the tsunami was less violent. It formed a whirlpool in one harbor, flowing around and around until the fish in the water got dizzy and were easy to catch.

Tiny bits of ash from Krakatoa floated high in the air all the way around the world. Wherever the ash went, it made the sky look very strange for a while. In one city the sunset was so red that firemen drove around looking for a fire. In some places the ash made the sun look sickly green. And in China people were terrified when the moon came up blue.

LOST CITIES

More than 1,900 years ago, a thick cloud of hot ash and gas suddenly darkened the city of Pompeii (pronounced pom-PAY) in Italy. Mount Vesuvius was erupting. No one had suspected that Vesuvius was a volcano; people were confused and not sure what to do. Many who decided the cloud was dangerous hurried to escape in boats. When ash and chunks of pumice began to fall, others tied pillows on their heads and ran away as fast as they could. A few tried to hide in cellars. Men and women who couldn't bear to leave their possessions behind spent time packing up money, gold, jewels, silver plates, even mirrors. One little girl kept trying to lead her terrified horse away. But by now it was too late. Everyone who had not left Pompeii died from breathing the hot, poisonous gases that blew into the city. Ash more than 30 feet deep soon buried them all.

Meanwhile, an immense storm began in the cloud over Vesuvius. Rain, mixed with ash, formed a kind of mud that streamed down the mountain, away from Pompeii and toward a city called Herculaneum (pronounced her-cue-LAY-nee-um). Many people were trapped and drowned in the flood. Before it stopped, every street and building in Herculaneum lay under mud more than 50 feet deep.

After a while, grass and trees took root in the bare but fertile volcanic soil that covered the two cities. Farmers moved in and planted crops. New towns grew up and people forgot about the old ones.

For seventeen centuries the two lost cities stayed lost. Who found them at last? Canal diggers were shoveling down through layers of ash when they uncovered a corner of Pompeii. A farmer who had never heard of Herculaneum decided he needed a better, deeper well. His digging turned up stones from an ancient building. This started more digs that uncovered Herculaneum itself.

At first, treasure hunters tunneled through the ash that had packed down and hardened. Lucky ones found statues, gold rings, bracelets, coins, gold and silver cups. Finally, museums and the government of Italy began serious digging. With shovels, scoops and drills, whole crews of excavators cleared the ash away.

This enormous job has been going on for more than a hundred years, and it is still not even half-finished. But it has been worth the trouble. It uncovered many beautiful things—and many surprises. Lovely paintings, not much harmed by the ash, still decorated the walls of rich people's homes. On other walls, adults and children had scratched all sorts of messages: *If you don't study, teacher will whack you.* *Beware of the dog.* *Don't litter.* *Vibius slept here.* For 1,900 years, the ash had preserved cakes and loaves of bread in bakers' ovens. A dish of eggs, unbroken, still sat on a table. So did a lunch of chicken, fish, bread and fruit.

When excavators started digging out Pompeii, they found strange holes in the hardened ash. Where did the holes come from? People who couldn't escape in time had been completely buried in the ash, which packed down around them. When the bodies decayed, hollow places were left. One of the men who was doing excavation used the hollows as molds. He poured in liquid plaster and waited until it hardened. Then he scraped off the ash. What he had made was a kind of plaster statue that showed exactly what each person looked like. Dozens of these molds now tell how people in Pompeii dressed and did their hair, and how they were sitting or standing or lying the moment the ash buried them.

More than any other places, the two lost cities have told what life was like long ago. We can look inside houses, shops, even a hotel, where tourists wrote their names on the walls of their rooms. We know that some people were neat, but others, after lunch, just tossed their chicken bones on the ground in the garden. We even know what the family in one house read, although their books were damaged and the ink has turned light gray.

THE RING OF FIRE

There are a lot of active volcanoes in the world—about 600 of them. Scientists call them active because each one has erupted at least once in the last 5,000 years. Most of them can be found in a long chain around the edges of the Pacific Ocean. Others form shorter chains in several different places.

Why aren't they scattered here and there all over the Earth? No one really knew until about thirty years ago. The answer is so surprising that at first scientists found it hard to believe. It turns out that the Earth's surface, including the continents and the ocean floor, is made up of vast slabs of rock called *tectonic plates*. There are seven big ones and a number of smaller ones. The plates are on the average about 60 miles thick and are made of solid rock. They float on top of a layer of hot, partly melted rock. Amazingly, they don't just stay in place. The soft, melted

layer is slippery enough so that the plates can move around on it like rafts on a lake, only very, very slowly—just a few inches a year at most.

As they move, the plates slide past one another, pull apart, or bump into each other. At the edges of plates, where the bumping and the pulling take place, most of the volcanoes in the world appear.

How do the colliding plates cause volcanoes? Where two plates have bumped into each other, the heavier plate bends and actually slides under the lighter one. After the edge of the heavier plate has been forced down fifty or so miles beneath the surface of the Earth, it starts to melt and turn into magma. Because it's a liquid, magma is lighter than solid rock. And so it slowly rises, melting and pushing its way to the surface. Finally, it bursts out in a volcanic eruption.

Volcanoes also erupt where plates are

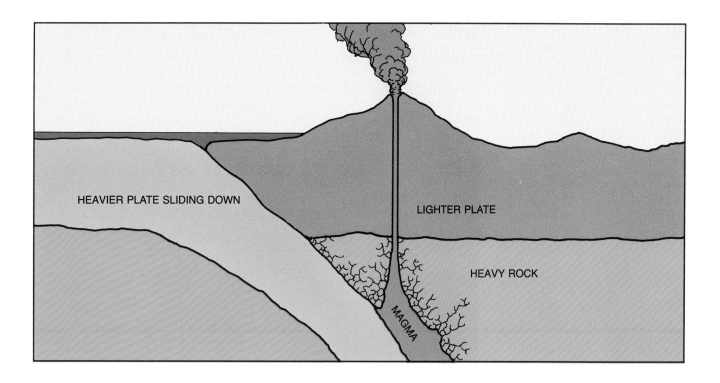

HEAVIER PLATE SLIDING DOWN

LIGHTER PLATE

HEAVY ROCK

MAGMA

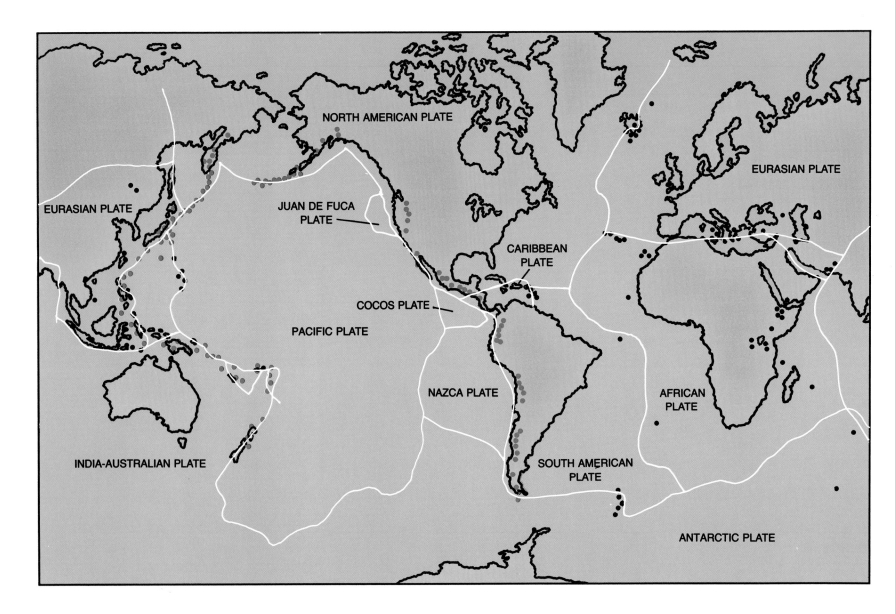

So many volcanoes occur around the rim of the Pacific Ocean that the chain they form is called the *Ring of Fire.* These volcanoes are represented by the red dots in the diagram above. Black dots represent other major volcanoes.

pulling apart. The North American plate is creeping away from the European plate at the rate of about an inch a year. The crack, or *rift*, between the two is in the middle of the Atlantic Ocean. As the two plates pull apart, magma from the molten layer below gushes up and fills the rift.

So much molten rock has erupted through the rift that it has created an enormous mountain range under the Atlantic Ocean. In fact, the entire ocean floor between Europe and America is made up of volcanic rock that filled the growing gap between the two continents. Volcanoes frequently erupt along the rift, but they are almost always far under the ocean. The only ones that have broken the surface are those in Iceland and the tiny island of Tristan da Cunha in the southern Atlantic Ocean.

The Pacific plate is a gigantic slab of rock that lies beneath the entire Pacific

Ocean. The plates on all sides of the Pacific plate are colliding with it, pulling away from it, or grinding past it. Almost all the way around it so many volcanoes have been formed that its rim is called the Ring of Fire.

How did anyone figure out that the continents are drifting around? One person to have the idea was a scientist who noticed something peculiar when he studied a map of the world. He saw that if he could push North America over toward Europe and South America toward Africa, the continents would fit together. This made him wonder. Was all the dry land in the world once an enormous single mass that split up into continents that slowly drifted apart?

After a while he became convinced that this was so. And he gave the original single continent a name—Pangaea (pronounced pan-GEE-ah). At first, most scientists did not believe his theory and called him a crackpot. But many years later they decided he was right.

The continents are the top parts of some of the plates; and when the plates move, the continents do, too. But what makes the plates move? No one really knows. Some scientists think the plates, like great thick rafts, are pushed around by currents in the molten rock under the Earth's crust. And what makes the rock under the crust so hot that it can flow? That, too, is a mystery. Scientists have thought of several different explanations. One idea is that the heat is caused by radioactive minerals deep inside the Earth.

These four drawings show the original *Pangaea* (upper left), the slow drifting of the continents over millions of years, and the continents as they appear today (lower right).

EARTHQUAKES—HOW AND WHY

One spring day in Los Angeles, a boy sat at a table on his porch eating Jell-O. Suddenly, the porch began to shake. The Jell-O seemed to pick itself up and hop out of the bowl. Then it hopped off the table onto the floor. The shaking got worse, and the boy ran out onto the sidewalk. Just as he came to a fireplug, the ground began to heave and roll. He wrapped his arms around the plug and hung on tight until the heaving stopped. He had lived through his first earthquake.

The Jell-O-bouncing quake wasn't a bad one. Really bad ones can tear huge gashes in the earth, heave boulders into the air, crack glaciers, and shake whole cities down in seconds. But what causes earthquakes? For a long time, scientists weren't sure. Some thought underground explosions were to blame. Others thought that quakes, like volcanoes, were caused by the movement of magma far below the Earth's surface. Arguments were still going on when, in 1891, a giant earthquake struck Japan.

This quake destroyed almost 200,000 houses. In a narrow strip 50 miles long, not one building was left undamaged and most were shaken to pieces. The ground shifted in peculiar ways. One long section of earth popped up 13 feet higher than the ground opposite it. Here and there, other sections were completely twisted. In one person's garden two old persimmon trees had faced each other east to west before the quake. Afterward, the trees faced each other north to south.

When the quake was over, a scientist named Bunjiro Koto went out to look at the damage. He was especially impressed

by the cracks and the strangely shifted rock that he found. Before long he had worked out a remarkable theory. Koto said it is actually the sudden breaking and slipping of rock that causes earthquakes. When great blocks of solid rock suddenly shift, they create waves of violent shaking and heaving. The rock breaks along cracks that scientists call *faults*. A fault isn't just a shallow split in the ground. It can go down dozens of miles, and may not appear on the surface at all.

Eventually, all scientists agreed that Koto was right. The breaking and shifting of rock is what causes earthquakes. But what makes rock break and shift? Koto didn't have the answer. Scientists now think the main cause is the movement of tectonic plates. As a plate creeps, one side of it may press and grind against a neighboring plate while a different side is diving beneath still another plate. This slow but powerful motion can stretch and strain rock until it suddenly breaks and snaps back with a terrible jolt. The 1891 quake in Japan was started by the Pacific plate sliding down under the Asian plate.

The shaking in an earthquake can go in waves from side to side, straining and stretching the earth with a snakelike motion that twists fences and even bends railroad tracks. Or the waves can go up and down. It was the up-and-down kind that made the boy's Jell-O hop out of its bowl. Most quakes have some of both kinds of wave. An earthquake that struck in a part of India called Assam had an especially powerful up-and-down motion. Fence posts popped straight up out of the ground. A chunk of rock the size of a chair was tossed so high that it broke in two when it landed.

In a quake in California in 1872, the up-and-down motion bounced fish out of the

Owens River onto the bank. Two men building a boat along the river saw the fish fly out, picked them up, and cooked them for breakfast. People who lived through that quake said chairs, tables and dishes leaped up and down as if they were alive.

Some earthquake waves move far below the surface of the Earth. Others move at the surface and make the ground ripple like waves on the ocean. Early one morning a forest ranger in Hawaii felt the first shudder of a quake. He jumped out of his pickup truck and sat on the ground. From where he sat he saw foot-high ripples coming toward him across an empty parking lot. In the earthquake at Assam, a long train of waves rippled through rice fields as fast as a person jogging. Sometimes surface waves move every which way, like a choppy sea, and people caught in the quake get seasick.

If a quake is very large, the waves can travel for thousands of miles—all the way through the Earth, in fact. A giant quake that struck Lisbon, Portugal, in 1755 made chandeliers swing back and forth in the great cathedrals all over Europe. And 1,000 miles away, a man in England reported that the shock tore a crack 150 yards long in his field.

Shortly after the quake struck at Assam, water began lapping against the banks of a reservoir in Burma 330 miles away. At first people thought the waves were caused by an elephant taking a bath, but where was the elephant? The motion of the water turned out to be a *seiche*—a kind of sloshing started by earthquake waves. The Lisbon quake caused a seiche (pronounced *saysh*) that broke boats loose from their moorings in canals in Holland more than 1,000 miles away. And a quake in Alaska sloshed half the water out of a big swimming pool 3,000 miles away in Texas.

WHAT THE BEARS KNEW

Jim Bedingfield would never forget Good Friday, 1964. Just at sunset he was driving his pickup truck down a street in the town of Valdez in Alaska when the earth started to shake. Then ground waves, 3 feet high, rippled past him. Bells rang as the quake rocked Valdez's churches. Frightened, Jim leaped out of his truck. Suddenly, the earth opened beneath him and he fell into a deep crack. Jim was sure he was a goner. But an instant later, a huge jet of water squirted out of the crack, lifted him up, and set him down safely on the ground.

The Good Friday quake triggered large sea waves that smashed boats in Valdez's harbor. Oil tanks near the harbor broke open and set fire to most of the water-front. Cars and even airplanes bounced up and down on their tires. Outside the town, the quake bent railroad tracks back and forth like twin snakes wriggling across a field. When the quake ended, much of Valdez looked like a junkyard, with cracks in the streets and wrecked buildings everywhere.

The same quake also struck Anchorage, Alaska, where houses in one neighborhood had been built high on a hill overlooking the ocean. During the quake, they slid downhill and ended up in a wrecked jumble that stretched all the way to the beach below. What went on here?

Scientists who came to Anchorage examined the soil under the city and

solved the mystery. When the houses were built, the earth seemed solid and strong, even though it was quite wet. The trouble was that the ground had been formed in several layers. A layer of soft, wet clay was sandwiched between two layers of stiff clay. When the earthquake shook the ground, the soft, wet layer turned into a thick liquid! Now the stiff top layer, with its load of houses, began to float downhill on the liquid layer. Soon it broke up into islands separated by huge cracks. The islands leaned, lurched, and spilled down the hill. Families ran out into the snow, while their homes split apart and their cars turned over or were squashed by falling trees. Luckily, most people escaped.

The small fishing town of Cordova wasn't badly damaged by the earthquake, but it was left with a terrible problem. The quake raised the whole town about 7 feet, making the harbor much shallower. Now Cordova's fishing fleet could not bring the day's catch close enough to some of the canneries along the shore. Seldovia, another fishing town, had the opposite problem. It sank 3½ feet during the quake. This meant that the town's boardwalk and main street flooded twice a day when the tide came in.

The Good Friday quake began as the Pacific plate pushed beneath the North American continental plate. Earthquake waves traveled south from Alaska and made buildings sway in Seattle, 1,400 miles

away. When the waves reached Houston, 3,000 miles away, they lifted the entire city about 4 inches and then gently dropped it down again as they passed. Nobody in Houston felt even a bump. But scientists knew about the waves because their instruments detected them.

After the quake, scientists were eager to find out what changes it had caused in Alaska's coastline. With the help of barnacles—sea animals that live on rocks at sea level—one change was easy to spot. Barnacles turn white and die if they're out of water too long. When scientists checked the rocks along the shore, they saw a white line of dead barnacles several feet above the level of the sea. The line marked sea level before the quake struck. It told scientists that the Good Friday quake had lifted a large section of the Alaskan coast several feet higher than it had been. In fact, an area larger than the whole state of Illinois had been raised. But another area almost as large had sunk a few feet.

The Good Friday earthquake caught Alaskans completely by surprise; but the day before the quake, bears on Kodiak Island seemed to sense that something was about to happen. They woke up two weeks early from their long winter hibernation. Although they hadn't eaten in months and were extremely hungry, they didn't waste a minute looking for food. Instead, they ran as fast as they could away from the main earthquake area.

WHEN THE MISSISSIPPI FLOWED BACKWARD

The week before Christmas, in 1811, a tremendous earthquake terrified the pioneer families who lived near the Mississippi River. In the next two months other quakes followed, some as large as the first. The quakes struck near a town called New Madrid in Missouri. One old man who lived there said, "The ground rolled in waves a few feet high. By and by, these swells burst and threw up large volumes of water, sand and even coal."

Some of the cracks in the ground were 10 feet wide and went on for miles. The early settlers who lived in the area worried that one might open up and swallow somebody. But what could they do? The cracks, they noticed, always ran in the same direction—roughly north to south. So they cut down the tallest trees they could find, always dropping them so they lay east to west. Now when a quake hit, people would jump onto the nearest tree. If a crack opened up, anyone who got to a log in time wouldn't fall in.

Before the quakes ended, the banks of the Mississippi River collapsed for miles above and below New Madrid. Waterfalls and rapids formed in places where the river had flowed smoothly. Whole islands disappeared. Water sloshed from side to side, turned boats over, and washed men in canoes high onto land. After one shock, the river even flowed backward for a while. After another, church bells rang in Boston, half a continent away.

In some places around New Madrid, the earth rose up in huge domes. The quake left one flat area about the size of Manhattan Island 20 feet higher than it had been. Other areas sank. A stretch of forest in Tennessee 10 miles long fell 20 feet and filled with water. Today, it is called Reelfoot Lake. After all these years you can still see dead trees standing in the lake.

Scientists aren't really sure what caused the New Madrid quakes. The Mississippi River is far from any of the places where tectonic plates bump or scrape each other. Recently, scientists made very careful measurements that seem to show there are very ancient, very deep faults under the river. The rock along these great faults may have shifted and caused the New Madrid quakes. And they may do it again.

EARTHQUAKE COUNTRY

California is earthquake country. Many small quakes rattle the state every year. When a big one hit San Francisco in October 1989, thousands of fans were cheering the start of a world series baseball game. Suddenly, rows of seats rippled up and down like a roller coaster. No one in the stadium was hurt, but in nearby Oakland many people died when the top of a double-decker highway collapsed and crushed the cars below. The 1989 quake did a lot of damage, but an earlier one in April 1906 was much worse.

The night before it struck, Enrico Caruso, a famous opera singer, went to bed at the Palace Hotel in San Francisco. A little after 5 o'clock the next morning, a violent shaking waked him. The Great San Francisco Earthquake had just begun.

The shocks ended and then the ground rolled for five minutes. Caruso stood in a doorway to avoid falling plaster. As soon as the rolling stopped, he dressed and rushed out into the street. Fires had started in buildings nearby. Soon the Palace Hotel began to burn. Caruso wan-

dered about trying to decide what to do. In the center of the city, he found a crowd of people, moaning and crying. Perhaps, Caruso thought, he could do something to comfort them. He began to sing. The crowd grew quiet—for a while, at least.

Later Caruso made his way to the dock where a ferryboat took passengers across the bay to Oakland. Hundreds of people were already fighting for places on the next boat. Caruso pushed through to the guards and told them who he was. The Great Caruso—the world's greatest singer? The guards didn't believe him. But moments later, when Caruso sang again, they changed their minds. And of course they let him onto the boat.

Others were not so lucky. The earthquake killed hundreds of people and destroyed thousands of buildings. Some rocked and toppled over; some were shaken to bits. But most were burned in the fire that followed the quake. For three days the smoke was so thick that it was hard to tell day from night. Firemen could do nothing because the earthquake had broken all the water pipes.

San Francisco sits on the edge of the North American plate, where it jams up against the Pacific plate. The Pacific plate is sliding slowly north. The problem is that it doesn't slide just a little bit at a time. Instead, it gets stuck for years and then lurches forward several feet. This sets off powerful earthquake waves. The whole plate doesn't move all in one piece. During the 1906 quake, one section of it jumped northward as much as 20 feet. In other places it moved just a little.

This has been going on for millions of years, and you can see the result if you fly over western California. For 800 miles, in an almost straight line, the earth is disturbed along the break where the two plates rub together. This long break is called the San Andreas fault.

Earthquakes are a threat along the entire San Andreas fault. The largest quake in southern California hit near Los Angeles in 1857. The heaving, rolling ground made it impossible to stand up. The quake tore deep gashes in the ground, but not many people were hurt, because Los Angeles was just a small town in 1857. An old prospector who was camping on top of the fault jumped out of his bedroll when he felt the earth move. He turned around just in time to see a crack open up, swallow his camping gear, then close again.

PREDICTING EARTHQUAKES

The animal keepers at a zoo in China began to worry one morning in 1969. Why were the yaks not eating? Why did the swans refuse to go near the water? Why did a giant panda hold its head in its paws and scream? The keepers decided it was time to give a report to their city's special earthquake office. Sure enough, at noon a quake did happen not far away. Scientists in China, and in many other places, think that animals often act in unusual ways just before an earthquake. So people are asked to report any such strange behavior.

Can animals really tell when a quake is coming? There is no absolute proof that they can, but some scientists find it believable that various creatures do get warnings of some sort. Before quakes, people have seen hundreds of strange goings-on. Rats, they said, left buildings and ran wildly in the streets. Cats moved their kittens out of houses. Dogs barked and howled. Bats flew in the daytime. Elephants trumpeted. Bees left their hives. Tigers and other zoo animals would not go into their shelters. Pigeons flew continuously. A giant swarm of fireflies appeared. Pigs bit pigs. And ants brought their eggs up from nests underground.

How could animals know that an earthquake is about to happen? Perhaps some get alarmed because they are able to sense vibrations that people can't feel. Once, before a big quake in China, snakes that had been hibernating came out of their dens and then froze to death in the snow. Scientists think that underground rock movements somehow warmed the earth and fooled the snakes into acting as if spring had come.

There are other hints of trouble that scientists pay attention to. Some people feel seasick and get headaches a few hours before a quake. No one knows why. Before a quake, well water often contains more than the usual amount of a gas called radon. In parts of China where there have been many quakes, children bring samples of water to school for radon testing. Using many clues, Chinese scientists have accurately predicted ten earthquakes, and people were moved to safety before anything happened.

Scientists use instruments called *seismographs* to detect movements and vibrations in the ground. Seismographs are so sensitive that they record vibrations caused by the footsteps of nearby animals. Scientists can even tell if the animal was a horse or a cow or a pig!

Every year seismographs detect about a million quakes, but only about twenty of these are large ones. Even before the study of earthquakes became a science, people thought it was important to keep records of where and when they happened. In China, the first of these were written down twenty-seven centuries ago. Today scientists keep track of places where quakes often happen. This helps engineers plan where to put dams and reservoirs. Even more important, they discover where it is especially dangerous to build a nuclear power plant.

A seismograph measures the height of earthquake waves. The height tells scientists the size of a quake according to a system called the *Richter scale*. Measurements on the scale go in steps from 1 to 10. Earthquakes above 5.5 on the Richter scale can do serious damage. The largest quake in the twentieth century, which happened off the coast of South America in 1960, registered almost 9 on the Richter scale.

An earthquake that measures 9 on the scale is ten times more powerful than one that registers 8, which is ten times worse than one that measures 7, and so on. So the Good Friday quake in Alaska, which was about 8.5 on the Richter scale, was 10,000 times more powerful than a dishrattler in Boston that measured 4.5.

A quake doesn't have to be high on the scale to do a great deal of damage. "Earthquakes don't kill people, falling buildings do," said one scientist after a quake struck Armenia in the Soviet Union in 1988. The quake measured just 6.9 on the Richter scale, but it killed over 20,000 people, because many new buildings were poorly constructed and old ones made of stone fell apart.

People who live in earthquake country say you can tell how strong a quake is without the Richter scale. A mild one makes you stagger a little when you walk. A somewhat stronger one makes it hard to drive a car. Then it's hard to stand up; then impossible to steer a car; then the ground cracks open; then rails are bent slightly; then bent a lot. Finally, when things get tossed in the air, you know it's a really bad quake.

AND HERE'S MORE...

- The longest earthquake we know about lasted for three years, from 1870 to 1873. It jolted the earth in Greece 86,000 times—more than a hundred shocks a day.
- An earthquake under the Gobi Desert in Asia moved a whole mountain several yards to the east, then back west, then finally east again.
- The biggest volcano we know about is not on Earth but on the planet Mars. It is 16 miles high, and its caldera is 50 miles wide.
- In 1958 an earthquake set off a huge landslide at Lituya Bay, Alaska. Millions of tons of rock and ice fell thousands of feet into the bay, creating a wave that rose 1,740 feet! Scientists call this kind of wave a *swash*.

- Great ocean waves called tsunamis are started, along with earthquakes, when a chunk of the ocean floor suddenly drops down or pops up. Underwater landslides can also start tsunamis. These waves can cross oceans with amazing speed. One that struck the Hawaiian islands traveled from the coast of Alaska, 2,300 miles away, in less than five hours.

- The ash thrown out in eruptions is different for each volcano. It's like a fingerprint that can identify which volcano it came from.
- After Krakatoa erupted, people who lived on nearby islands said the volcano did only one good thing: It killed all the mosquitoes.
- Over a half-million years ago, a volcano erupted in the part of the United States now called Yellowstone National Park. The magma it left underground is still very hot. Now when water seeps down into the earth, it turns to steam and shoots back up in fountains of water droplets called *geysers*. The highest geyser in Yellowstone National Park sends water more than 200 feet into the air.

An even taller geyser, called Waimangu, in New Zealand once rose more than seven times as high. Waigmangu has stopped spouting, but steam from neighboring underground volcanic areas is being used to heat houses and to drive engines that make electric power.
- Volcanoes knock down trees, bury green fields in lava, and kill people. Still, what volcanoes have done isn't all bad. Think about this: Millions of years ago, when our planet was new, no living things grew anywhere. But volcanoes erupted constantly and water bubbled out of the magma. Some scientists think volcanoes provided the water that created oceans and the rain for plants and animals when life finally began to appear on Earth.

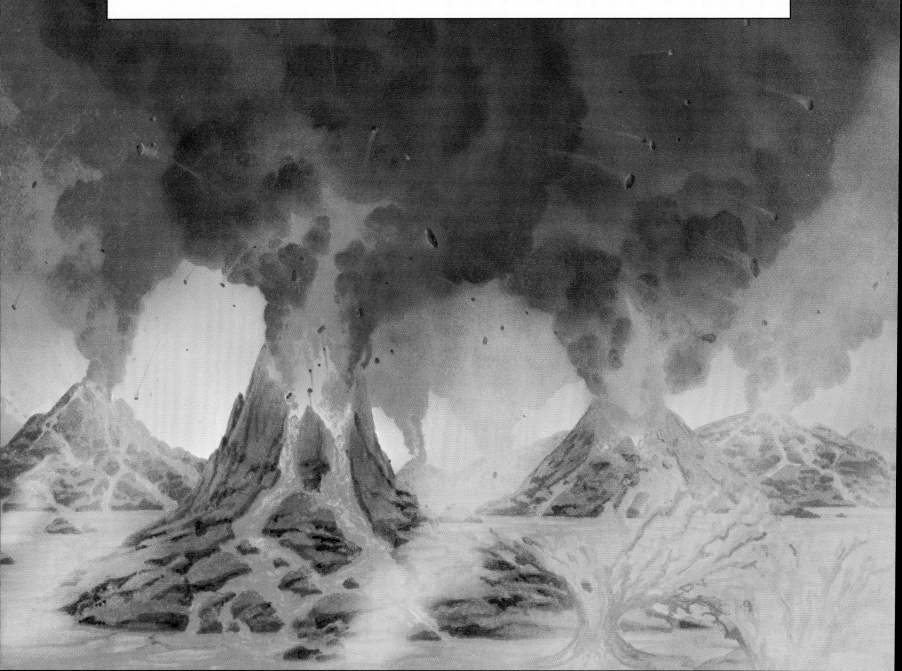

ACKNOWLEDGMENTS

The authors are very grateful to Professor Marty Godchaux of Mount Holyoke College for giving us a volcanologist's-eye view of our restless planet, for reading our manuscript, and for making valuable suggestions. We also want to thank Professor Alvin Cohen of the University of Massachusetts at Amherst, Michael Valentine, and the following young readers for their help: Maria Roeper, Emily Riddle, and Raphael Folsom.

SIMON AND SCHUSTER BOOKS FOR YOUNG READERS
Simon & Schuster Building, Rockefeller Center, 1230 Avenue of the Americas, New York, New York 10020.

Library of Congress Cataloging-in-Publication Data:
Elting, Mary, 1909- . Volcanoes and earthquakes / by Mary Elting ; illustrated by Courtney.
Summary: Discusses how earthquakes and volcanic eruptions occur and how they can be predicted.
1. Volcanoes—Juvenile literature. 2. Earthquakes—Juvenile literature. [1. Volcanoes. 2. Earthquakes.]
I. Courtney, ill. II. Title. QE521.3.E37 1990 551.2'1—dc20 89-37107 CIP AC
ISBN 0-671-67217-7.